# How Do I Get Rid Of a Ghost?

## GOING UP AGAINST THE SPIRIT WORLD

DAVID THOMASON

WESTBOW
PRESS
A DIVISION OF THOMAS NELSON

ISBN: 978-1-4497-1912-8 (e)
ISBN: 978-1-4497-1913-5 (sc)
ISBN: 978-1-4497-1914-2 (hc)
Library of Congress Control Number: 2011930697

WestBow Press books may be ordered through booksellers or by contacting:

WestBow Press
A Division of Thomas Nelson
1663 Liberty Drive
Bloomington, IN 47403
www.westbowpress.com
1-(866) 928-1240

Printed in the United States of America

WestBow Press rev. date: 6/17/2011

# Contents

∽

"THERE ARE MORE THINGS IN HEAVEN AND EARTH, HORATIO, THAN ARE DREMPT OF IN YOUR PHILOSOPY."

HAMLET by William Shakespeare

There are those individuals who don't believe in ghosts, demons, spirits, unseen entities or whatever you want to call them. To them I say, "The only reason you don't believe is because you've never experienced them." Once you see a black mass, hear voices in an empty house or see something move when no one was near it, you'll believe.

This book was written at the prompting of a good friend because of the experiences I've had dealing with 'things unseen' in homes I've lived in and in the homes of friends and family. I've known many people who have had something unexplainable in their homes and tried different ways to get rid of it themselves or with the help of a priest or pastor, sometimes with little or no success.

There are many people that are experiencing things right now and have no idea what's happening, have no idea what to do or where to turn. Some have tried different ways to get rid of ghosts and had no success or did have success, but whatever it was came back. The information in this book should answer many of the questions of what ghosts are and what to do about them.

This book is written for those who have something in their homes or know someone who does. It is also written for those who know the authority and power from God that lies within them but aren't sure how to use it. Tapping into that power is a wonderful thing, whether for ridding homes of ghosts or for any other ministry in which you may be involved.

My hope is that by the time you're done reading this book you'll have a good understanding of what ghosts are, where they came from, how they can be removed and by whom.

# CHAPTER 1

∾

## What Is A Ghost?

## Before Getting Into What A Ghost Is, Let's First Take A Look At What A Ghost Is Not...

If you ask people what a ghost is most would give the same answer. Most of the people I know have been raised with the idea that a ghost is the spirit of someone they loved that hasn't "passed on". Ok, maybe it's not a loved one, but it's someone.

The idea of a person who hasn't gone to heaven, hell, Valhalla or some other place, but rather "hangs around" came about 2500-2700 years ago, having its origins in ancient Greece. Most Catholics I know (I grew up in a predominately Catholic community) consider a person who has died, but wasn't good enough for heaven and not bad enough to go to hell, to be in Purgatory or "Limbo", although this is not an official doctrine of the Catholic Church. Many Catholics believe that some, if not all ghosts are those trapped in Limbo.

Many New Age religions teach that if someone passes away and doesn't "go into the light" they may be trapped here on Earth as a spirit. Not being able to "go into the light" can be caused by having unfinished business here on Earth or evil they have done while mortals. Supposedly, that evil must be atoned for before they can move on. But how does haunting someplace atone for anything?

I don't believe either of these theories. The Bible, for the most part, has been the oldest authority on things related to hauntings, demons and the afterlife. It teaches that:

> *And as it is appointed unto men once to die, but after this the judgment:*
>
> *Hebrews 9:27*

In this statement by the Apostle Paul, it would seem that we don't stick around for long once we die. Although there is nothing in the Bible about it, there seem to have been occasions in which a person who has passed away has been allowed to show themselves to someone for the purpose of saying "good-bye". I have heard several stories of this happening. One example of this is my own grandmother. My grandmother, a very strong Christian woman, passed away in Yucaipa, California. At the moment she died her son, my uncle, was living in Lancaster, Pennsylvania. He was awakened and saw her in his room. According to my uncle, she leaned and kissed him to tell him good-bye, then disappeared. He woke my aunt up and told her what he saw. My aunt said to him, "Oh, that's crazy, go back to sleep." Later that morning my father called him to tell him that my grandmother had passed away during the night.

According to Judaism, the soul of a person who dies will stay near the body for three days then go to God. In ancient times the family and friends would stay near the body for those three days in case the soul should re-enter the body and the person should wake up. This is thought to be the origin of the "Wake." In the Gospel of John, Chapter 11, Jesus waited for three days after the death of Lazarus before coming to raise him from the dead. Jesus waited so long on purpose to prove His deity, showing that even if the soul has gone to God He has the authority to bring it back and raise the dead.

## Ok, So If Ghosts Aren't Dead People, Then What Are They And Where Did They Come From?

In many hauntings, things start out mildly as a bump here, a rattle there, maybe some footsteps or soft, unexplainable voices in the night. In some cases things get worse as time goes on. What began as a benign poltergeist activity has become a very scary haunting with things moving and people being touched, poked or scratched.

In the movie *Paranormal Activity* (DreamWorks Films, 2009) this is exactly what happened, but taken to the extreme. What seemed to be a harmless ghost turned out to be a demon, a very powerful demon who was the cause of a murder/suicide. Although this is only a Hollywood movie, things like this have been documented.

The Bible is the oldest book known to talk about demons and their origins. According to Revelation 12:9, demons are the angels of Satan.

> And the great dragon was cast out, that old serpent, called the Devil, and Satan, which deceiveth the whole world: he was cast out into the earth, and his angels were cast out with him.
>
> Revelation 12:9

But why were they cast out? Lucifer, also known as the Devil, Satan, Beelzebub and by a host of other names, was at one time one of the highest and most beautiful angels of God. However his power and beauty went to his head bringing forth the very first sin, pride. Pride lead to his eviction from heaven and the damage to his ego brought about his hatred toward mankind.

*Thou hast been in Eden the garden of God; every precious stone was thy covering, the sardius, topaz, and the diamond, the beryl, the onyx, and the jasper, the sapphire, the emerald, and the carbuncle, and gold: the workmanship of thy tabrets and of thy pipes was prepared in thee in the day that thou wast created. Thou art the anointed cherub that covereth; and I have set thee so: thou wast upon the holy mountain of God; thou hast walked up and down in the midst of the stones of fire. Thou wast perfect in thy ways from the day that thou wast created, till iniquity was found in thee. By the multitude of thy merchandise they have filled the midst of thee with violence, and thou hast sinned: therefore I will cast thee as profane out of the mountain of God: and I will destroy thee, O covering cherub, from the midst of the stones of fire. Thine heart was lifted up because of thy beauty, thou hast corrupted thy wisdom by reason of thy brightness: I will cast thee to the ground, I will lay thee before kings, that they may behold thee.*

*Ezekiel 28:13 – 17*

*How art thou fallen from heaven, O Lucifer, son of the morning! How art thou cut down to the ground, which didst weaken the nations! For thou hast said in thine heart, I will ascend into Heaven, I will exalt my throne above the stars (angels) of God: I will sit also upon the mount of the congregation, in the sides of the north: I will ascend above the heights of the clouds; I will be like the most High.*

*Isaiah 14:12 – 14*

There are two things to note in these passages. First, Ezekiel 28: 13 and 15 state that Satan was created. He is not the creator as he has led many to believe. God made Lucifer to be perfect, the highest and most beautiful angel. This leads us to the second point. In the passage from Isaiah, Lucifer, having a free will, as do all creations of God, decided he was as beautiful and powerful as God was. He wanted to be equal with his creator. He must have been very persuasive because when God threw Lucifer out of heaven one third of the angels followed him.

*And his tail drew the third part of the stars of heaven, and did cast them to the earth:*

*Revelation 12:4*

For the remainder of this book the terms ghost and demon will be interchangeable since they truly are one and the same.

## If Satan Is So Powerful That He Could Fool Angels, Why Is He Messing With Humans?

At some point in time, prior to the creation of Adam and Eve, Satan was told that he was not going to be the most beautiful or most powerful angel forever. God decided to create an entire race that would have a higher position than Lucifer. This race was not to be angels, but would be called God's children. Because of his pride and jealousy, the subjugation and destruction of mankind became the prime goal of Satan and his minions.

*Know ye not that we shall judge angels?*

*1Corinthians 6:3*

If we are going to judge angels, both heavenly and fallen, then we must do so from a point of higher authority. For those who already have a relationship with Jesus, that authority has ALREADY been given!

*And the seventy (Disciples of Jesus) returned again with joy, saying, Lord, even the devils are subject unto us through thy name. And he said unto them, I beheld Satan as lightning fall from heaven. Behold, I give unto you power to tread on serpents and scorpions, and over all the power of the enemy: and nothing shall by any means hurt you. Notwithstanding in this rejoice not, that the spirits are subject unto you; but rather rejoice, because your names are written in heaven.*

*Luke 10:17 – 20*

In this passage of Luke, the serpents and scorpions that we now have power to tread upon are not literal snakes and scorpions, but rather demons and Satan. Remember the Garden of Eden? Satan dropped by to talk with Eve in the form of a serpent.

The fact is that WE are a prize in the eyes of both God and Satan. Humans were created by God to have a relationship with Him higher than that of angels. Those who call upon God literally become His children by adoption. Although the angels have a loving relationship with God, they are never called His children.

*For as many as are led by the Spirit of God, these are sons of God. For ye received not the spirit of bondage again unto fear; but ye received the spirit of adoption, whereby we cry, Abba, Father.*

*Romans 8:14-15*

*but when the fullness of the time came, God sent forth his Son, born of a woman, born under the law, that he might redeem them that were under the law, that we might receive the adoption of sons. And because ye are sons, God sent forth the Spirit of his Son into our hearts, crying, Abba, Father. So that thou art no longer a bondservant, but a son; and if a son, then an heir through God.*

The word *Abba* is the Hebrew word for father, or more literally, daddy. God wants a heartfelt relationship with us, not a formal relationship. Not only are we God's children, but we are His heirs! As heirs we have all the power of the Creator of the Universe at our disposal through the working of the Holy Spirit!

Lucifer is jealous of the position we have with God. In the eyes of Satan we are a prize to be destroyed. He wants the human race eliminated to keep us from having that place in Heaven higher than he once held.

*Be sober, be vigilant; because your adversary the devil, as a roaring lion, walketh about, seeking whom he may devour:*

## Why Do Demons Pretend To Be People That Have Died?

Because of Satan's jealousy of humanity, he will do all he can to keep us away from a relationship with God. He uses drugs, alcohol, anger, hatred, conceit, power, self pity and a host of other things to keep us away from a God who loves us.

The Devil has one basic tactic to get our eyes off of God, lies. Satan has lied to all of us, making us think we are not worthy of being children of God or trying to make us think that God and Satan don't exist. I have known far too many people who have told me they have done things 'God just can't forgive me for'. This has been one of Satan's biggest lies! The Bible tells us:

> I acknowledge my sin unto thee, And mine iniquity did I not hide:
> I said, I will confess my transgressions unto Jehovah; And thou forgavest the iniquity of my sin.

Psalm 32:5

> If we confess our sins, he is faithful and righteous to forgive us our sins, and to cleanse us from all unrighteousness.

1 John 1:9

Don Francisco got it right in his song "I Don't Care Where You've Been Sleeping" on the album *Forgiven (1977)*. Part of the lyrics tell us…"I *don't care where you've been sleeping. I don't care who's made your bed. I already gave my life to set you free. There's no sin you can imagine that is stronger than my love, if you'll come home again to me.*"

The fact is that God can, and will, forgive any sin we have ever committed, regardless of how bad WE think it is, if we are willing to confess that sin and, most importantly, ask for forgiveness.

Lucifer will send people to tempt us with drugs, alcohol, power, etc. making us think we don't need God, that God hates us, that God isn't interested or that God doesn't exist. He will do anything to make us believe there is something other than heaven or hell waiting for us after we die. This includes sending many of his fallen angels to act as though they are the dead coming back as spirits. Through this lie many New Age religions have been created and he has convinced millions that God does not exist. Jesus Himself says in this passage from the Gospel of John, Satan is the father of lies.

*You belong to your father the devil, and you want to carry out the desires of your father. He was a murderer from the beginning and has never stood by the truth, since there is no truth in him. Whenever he tells a lie he speaks in character, for he is a liar and the father of lies.*

*John 8:44*

Satan has used many in his army of fallen angels to convince people that if someone passes away from a tragedy, trauma or has 'unfinished business' that his spirit will remain on Earth. Demons have been around a very long time, are spirits and don't have bodies that wear out and die as we do. They are also very intelligent and it is common belief in Christianity that many of them can, and are, assigned to individuals as are guardian angels from God.

*For he will give his angels charge over thee, To keep thee in all thy ways.*

*Psalm 91:11*

*See that ye despise not one of these little ones; for I say unto you, that in heaven their angels do always behold the face of my Father who is in heaven.*

*Matthew 18:10*

From these verses we can see that God has assigned guardian angels to watch over you your entire life. Why then can't Satan assign a demon to follow us and try to deceive us our whole lives? Since a demon can have knowledge of a person from their birth until death, it seems likely that that demon could easily assume that persona after death, making it seem as if the deceased has returned as a spirit and is haunting the person's former home, apartment, office, etc.

Demons pretend to be the 'disembodied spirits of the dearly departed' in an effort to deceive us about the truth that is waiting for us when we pass on. Demons certainly don't want us believe that the fate of those not having a relationship with Jesus is with them in hell. They want to make us think there is something other than hell or that there is a place where those who weren't good enough for heaven or bad enough for hell can go to pay their penance and earn their way into heaven. However, the Bible teaches that heaven and hell are real places and that once a person dies, there is no 'hanging around'.

> And inasmuch as it is appointed unto men once to die, and after this cometh judgment;
>
> Hebrews 9:27

> And be not afraid of them that kill the body, but are not able to kill the soul: but rather fear him who is able to destroy both soul and body in hell.
>
> Matthew 10:28

> Blessed be the God and Father of our Lord Jesus Christ, who according to his great mercy begat us again unto a living hope by the resurrection of Jesus Christ from the dead, unto an inheritance incorruptible, and undefiled, and that fadeth not away, reserved in heaven for you,
>
> 1Peter 1:3-4

# CHAPTER 2

∾

## *Legal Rights Of Ghosts*

## What Is Sin And How Does It Give Demons Rights?

It may seem like an odd concept, but ghosts (demons) have certain rights. These rights are given to them by us, not God! A demon can receive the right to live in or enter a place or a person as the result of sin or trauma. The rights a demon has over a person or place can also be transferred from one generation to the next.

Sin is defined as: *A concept of acts that violate a moral rule. Commonly, the moral code of conduct is decreed by a divine entity* (God).

God's moral code is commonly referred to as the Ten Commandments or The Law. The basic rules of this code are found in Exodus 20: 3-17. The typical condensed version is…

1)  *Thou shalt have no other gods before Me.*

2)  *Thou shalt not make unto thee a graven image.*

3)  *Thou shalt not take the name of God in vain.*

4)  *Remember the sabbath day, to keep it holy.*

5)  *Honor thy father and thy mother.*

6)  *Thou shalt not kill.*

7)  *Thou shalt not commit adultery.*

8)  *Thou shalt not steal.*

9)  *Thou shalt not bear false witness against thy neighbor.*

10) *Thou shalt not covet thy neighbor's house, thou shalt not covet thy neighbor's wife, nor his man servant, nor his maid-servant, nor his ox, nor his ass, nor anything that is thy neighbor's.*

In Galatians Chapter 5:19-21 is a list of 'sins of the flesh'.

*Now the works of the flesh are manifest, which are these; Adultery, fornication, uncleanness, lasciviousness, Idolatry, witchcraft, hatred, variance, emulations, wrath, strife, seditions, heresies, Envyings, murders, drunkenness, revellings, and such like: of the which I tell you before, as I have also told you in time past, that they which do such things shall not inherit the kingdom of God.*

*because by the works of the law shall no flesh be justified in his sight; for through the law cometh the knowledge of sin.*

*Romans 3:20*

*Jesus answered them, Verily, verily, I say unto you, Every one that committeth sin is the bondservant of sin.*

*John 8:34*

The Bible tells us that God considers any violation of these rules to be sin. Not only does violating these rules bring spiritual death but also grants a legal right to Satan and his fallen angels over a person by the violator, thus making him a bondservant. A bondservant is a slave who is bound to service to his master to repay a debt (a bond). If you are a slave, you must have a master. Once a right is granted, a demon can now oppress or possess a person, place or object. A variety of rights can be granted over a person. Alcoholism, drug abuse, sexual abuse, violent behavior, murder, depression, insanity and child abuse are just a few of the areas rights can be held by demons over someone. When it comes to places such as houses, apartments and even objects, these same rights can apply.

Granted, property and objects cannot violate these laws, but someone who commits acts of sin in a place or that use an object to commit sin, grants a right to a demon over that place or object. People who have a demon are called "possessed", places that have demons living there are called "haunted" and objects that demons have Rights to are most often called "cursed."

*(for all these abominations have the men of the land done, that were before you, and the land is defiled);*

*Leviticus 18:27*

*Moreover the word of Jehovah came unto me, saying, Son of man, when the house of Israel dwelt in their own land, they defiled it by their way and by their doings:*

*Ezekiel 36:16- 17*

*Neither shalt thou bring an abomination (Idol) into thine house, lest thou be a cursed thing like it: but thou shalt utterly detest it, and thou shalt utterly abhor it; for it is a cursed thing. (Parenthesis added for clarification)*

*Deuteronomy 7:26*

Some objects most people consider "cursed" are Ouija boards, Tarot cards, Voodoo dolls and the like. However, any object can be cursed. I once heard about a piano that was cursed by a former owner. A couple bought the piano and soon after it was moved into their home the couple started having feelings of anger toward each other, nearly causing them to divorce. Once the piano was removed from the home everything returned to normal. Supposedly the tomb of King Tutankhamen was cursed, bringing about odd and tragic deaths to the men who opened the tomb.

A friend of mine asked me to come into a room of a house that she and her roommate were forced to turn into a storage room. It had been a guest bedroom when they first rented the house. Several guests that stayed in that particular room would end up on the sofa in the living room by morning. They complained of a 'weird feeling of fear' in the room. When I entered the room, the Lord impressed on me that there had been physical abuse on a child and that three demons had been granted the right to live in that room because of that abuse. Fear, Anger and Abuse were the demons that guests had been feeling. My friend and I prayed together and commanded the demons of Fear, Anger and Abuse and any other demons residing in that house to leave, in Jesus name. The demons left. Since that time the room has become a guest room again with no more complaints.

> *Therefore, as through one man (Adam) sin entered into the world, and death through sin; and so death passed unto all men, for that all sinned*

> *Romans 5:12*

> *Jehovah (God) is slow to anger, and abundant in lovingkindness, forgiving iniquity and transgression; and that will by no means clear the guilty, visiting the iniquity of the fathers upon the children, upon the third and upon the fourth generation.*

> *Numbers 14:18*

The rights granted by us to demons can be passed from one generation to the next. This most often happens at birth and will affect both parent and children. This transfer of rights is commonly referred to as a *generational curse*. As we read in Numbers 14:18, the iniquity of the fathers will fall upon their children unto the third and fourth generation. The third and fourth generation is not a maximum, but rather a minimum. It has become common knowledge in our society that if a parent is an alcoholic, drug abuser or abusive; his or her children will most likely grow up to be alcoholics, drug abusers or abusive over several generations.

Generational curses can be passed for hundreds of years and can often cause family illnesses that are passed on from parent to child.

One example of a generational curse involves a friend of mine. She had gone to a prayer group and during the time everyone was praying together my friend started feeling ill and began speaking in German, although she had never learned to speak German. When she got home she started asking her family about their history. She found that she had a German ancestor that had been cursed about 400 years ago! She went back to the group with this information and broke the curse. As a result of breaking that curse she and her daughter, who hadn't known any of this at the time, were healed of a physical illness that they were told by doctors was a genetic ailment that had plagued their family as far back as they could remember.

## How Can Traumatic Events Give Demons Rights?

When it comes to ghosts haunting a particular place or cursing an object, the same concepts apply. As mentioned earlier, if a sin has been committed this will give a demon or demons the right to live in the place the sins occurred or the items that were used. This seems to be a common theme in hauntings shown by ghost hunting groups on television and the many books on the subject.

Murder, abuse and rape are obviously traumatic occurrences. In many hauntings the sin is replayed again and again by the ghosts, sometimes often or sometimes only on the anniversary of the offence.

Two Stories…

A former supervisor of mine told me he was working one evening cleaning up around an empty house, getting it ready to sell. He happened to look in one of the windows through the bottom of a partially closed blind. What he saw scared him beyond words. He watched as a man used a knife to kill a woman as she lay on a bed. He put her into a box and removed her body from the home. My supervisor called the police immediately. When the police arrived they found the house completely empty with no blinds, no bed and no blood. One of the detectives looked into the history of the house and found that what my supervisor saw had actually occurred more than 30 years before on that date!

When I was 18 years old I worked for the Palmdale School District in California as a substitute custodian. One evening I was cleaning the north wing of an elementary school. I kept hearing footsteps in the hallway as I was cleaning the classrooms. Every time I went to see who it was, no one was there. However, one particular outside door would be unlocked and ajar. I checked and double checked and rechecked that lock to make sure it was working properly. I then checked all of the classrooms to make sure there was no one in the building. By the time I finished checking all the classrooms, the door was open again! This happened several times as I was working. When I told my manager what was happening he said "Oh! You've met our ghost!" He told me that in the 1960's a child had been crushed to death as students were trying to get out of that door and it jammed. The lock had been changed 3 times that he knew of and the door would not remain closed.

Any place that a sin or traumatic event has happened, a demon can be granted the right to live there and 'haunt' as it feels led to.

*"Defile not ye yourselves in any of these things: for in all these the nations are defiled which I cast out before you: And the land is defiled: therefore I do visit the iniquity thereof upon it, and the land itself vomiteth out her inhabitants...* **(For all these abominations have the men of the land done, which were before you, and the land is defiled;)"** (Emphasis added)

*Leviticus 18:24-25,27*

*And he cried mightily with a strong voice, saying, Babylon the great is fallen, is fallen,* **and is become the habitation of devils, and the hold of every foul spirit,** *and a cage of every unclean and hateful bird.* (Emphasis added)

*Revelation 18:2*

# CHAPTER 3

⤳

## Can Ghosts Hurt You?

Many people believe that ghosts are spiritual beings that are incapable of interacting with humans on a physical level. Nothing could be further from the truth. There have been hundreds of documented cases in which ghosts have made physical contact with people.

Most hauntings are usually just weird feelings, as in the story of my friend's spare room. Demons have been known to move objects and touch people who entered possessed homes. On a few episodes of a popular weekly ghost hunting documentary, ghosts have struck the leaders of the group on their backs and necks hard enough to leave marks and scratches. This has happened more than once on the program. One cameraman was shoved hard enough to knock him over and leave his face reddened by 'something unseen'.

> And behold, a man from the multitude cried, saying, Teacher, I beseech thee to look upon my son; for he is mine only child: behold, a spirit taketh him, and he suddenly crieth out; and it teareth him that he foameth, and it hardly departeth from him, bruising him sorely. And I besought thy disciples to cast it out; and they could not. And Jesus answered and said, O faithless and perverse generation, how long shall I be with you, and bear with you? bring hither thy son. And as he was yet a coming, the demon dashed him down, and tare him grievously. But Jesus rebuked the unclean spirit, and healed the boy, and gave him back to his father.
>
> Luke 9:38 -42

Probably the most famous haunting in the United States took place in Amityville, NY. The facts in the case are that in 1974, Ronald De Feo was the eldest son in a family of 5 children. He heard voices that told him to kill his family as they slept. Unfortunately he listened to the demonic voices. He shot and killed both of his parents and his 4 younger siblings. He is now serving 6 consecutive life sentences. In November of 1975 the

Lutz family bought and moved into the house. They claimed that they had several paranormal experiences and they abandoned the house in January of 1976. There is some controversy about the events the Lutz family experienced, but it is true that a family was murdered by demons acting through Ronald De Feo.

I was on a business trip in early 2010 and received a phone call from a very close relative in a near panic. She told me that the prior night, her 12 year old grandson was staying with her and her husband. According to the grandson, during the night something invisible shoved his head into his pillow, trying to suffocate him and told him "Come with me." This child is a close relative and I know him well. He's not given to making things up or lying. He managed to cry out loud enough to wake the grandfather. As the grandfather came into the room the entity let go of the grandson. As soon as I returned home, she, her husband and I forced the demon to leave by the power in Jesus name.

The friend who encouraged me to write this book has a twenty two year old son. She told me that "something" was scratching her son across his back and legs during the night. Whatever it was had left what she described to me as claw marks and welts. Even after seeing the marks and ruling out any logical scientific or medical reasons for them, her husband is unable to explain the cause of the scratches and refuses to believe that ghosts/demons are real and could be the reason for the marks. Here are her words about what happened...

"Before my son was scratched, he heard noises in his closet and low voices. Then he said he was hit on the shoulder from behind. Then weeks later is when he woke up with scratches. Let's put it this way, it scared him enough to go on line and order a "Blessed Crucifix". He was led to believe that this would make it stop. It only stopped when my son told me about it and I took the Bible up into his room and read the Lord's prayer, prayed and said 'leave in Jesus name' like you had suggested I do."

During our several conversations she told me her son also hung some rosary beads up in his room and the scratches stopped for a few months and the family isn't even Catholic! During our conversations I explained to her much of what is now in this book. Since the day she and her son went into his room and forced the entity to leave in Jesus name, her son has not had any more marks on his body or heard any noises or voices from his closet.

Yes, ghosts can hurt people!

# CHAPTER 4

∾

## Do Ancient Rituals Work To Get Rid Of Ghosts?

# Wicca

The name Wicca is a derivative form of an ancient word for a male witch. Another derivative of this ancient word is warlock. Wikipedia, an online encyclopedia, defines Wicca as *"a Neopagan religion and a form of modern witchcraft. It is often referred to as Witchcraft or 'the Craft' by its adherents, who are known as Wiccans or Witches. Wicca is typically a duo-theistic religion, worshipping a Goddess and a God, who are traditionally viewed as the Triple Goddess and the Horned God."*

A Horned god....who does that remind you of? I have been told by a practitioner of Wicca that their followers worship the Mother Goddess and they are not witches. But when one takes a hard look at Wicca one sees far too many rituals, teachings and practices to call it anything other than witchcraft.

Wicca is a very personalized religion. Not only is there the goddess and horned god, but the ALL or ONE. The ALL/ONE is an impersonal entity that is the creator of the goddess and has no personal contact with humanity. In his book *What's the Deal with Wicca?* [1] Steve Russo gives a rather accurate description of the ALL.

> [1] *The ALL/ONE is basically a huge melting pot of all the gods everyone in the world has ever thought of or believed in. The ALL/ONE is not male or female, has no body or real personality. It's more like a blender that you've dumped all the beliefs of the world into and crushed them together.*

Along with the ALL, the goddess and the horned god, the Wicca practitioner 'creates' and names his own gods to worship! These are often represented by stones, pieces of wood, crystals, clay figures, figurines, gold or silver objects and any number of other items. These gods receive all of their power from the person who created them. Wiccans often call upon these gods (idols) to do their bidding using rituals, chants, mantras and spells to help them with problems the Wiccan needs help with because they can't get out of a situation by themselves. The big question I have is "how can a god that someone has created from his own imagination have more power than the person who created it?" Here's what the Bible has to say about these 'created' gods:

> They are like a palm-tree, of turned work, and speak not: they must needs be borne (carried), because they cannot go (walk). Be not afraid of them; for they cannot do evil, neither is it in them to do good.

> (parenthesis added for clarification)     *Jeremiah 10:5*

> Shall a man make unto himself gods, which yet are no gods?

> *Jeremiah 16:20*

> for that they exchanged the truth of God for a lie, and worshipped and served the creature rather than the Creator, who is blessed for ever. Amen.

> *Romans 1:25*

The reality is that these 'gods' are really nothing but inanimate objects with no power to do anything!

Many Wiccans don't consider themselves witches even though they call on their home-made gods using the same spells as those who do call themselves witches. Many of these rituals and spells can be traced back for hundreds or even thousands of years. Many of those spells are used to call up 'entities' or spirits to help the Wiccan in particular situations. What kind of 'entities' or spirits are they? This will be discussed in detail in the section on mediums and shaman.

There are several rituals that have been used to remove ghosts and demons from people, places and things. They all have worked to some extent. However, often they just replace one entity with another and the latter condition is worse than the first. Jesus was accused by the religious leaders in His day of casting out demons by the power of Satan.

> But when the Pharisees heard it, they said, This man (Jesus) doth not cast out demons, but by Beelzebub the prince of the demons. (Satan)
>
> (Emphasis added)    Matthew 12:24

In response to this, Jesus reminded the rulers that

> ... Every kingdom divided against itself is brought to desolation; and every city or house divided against itself shall not stand: and if Satan casteth out Satan, he is divided against himself; how then shall his kingdom stand?
>
> Matthew 12:25 -26

If a witch or wiccan is trying to cast out a ghost/demon then it is certainly a house divided, commanding one demon to drive off another. Oftentimes, when a witch or wiccan casts out a ghost/demon, what's happening is they are either unknowingly replacing a demon of lower rank with one of a higher rank and with more power or they are adding more demons to the home, making things much worse.

# Catholic Exorcisms And House Blessings

According to the Catholic Encyclopedia, exorcism is:[1]

[1]*(1) the act of driving out, or warding off, demons, or evil spirits, from persons, places, or things, which are believed to be possessed or infested by them, or are liable to become victims or instruments of their malice.*

*(2) The means employed for this purpose, especially the solemn and authoritative adjuration of the demon, in the name of God, or any of the higher powers in which he is subject.*

Furthermore, the encyclopedia tells us that:

[1]*According to Catholic belief, demons or fallen angels retain their natural power, as intelligent beings, of acting on the material universe, and using material objects and directing material forces for their own wicked ends; and this power, which is in itself limited, and is subject, of course, to the control of Divine providence, is believed to have been allowed a wider scope for its activity in the consequence of the sin of mankind. Hence places and things as well as persons are naturally liable to diabolical infestation, within limits permitted by God, and exorcism in regard to them is nothing more than a prayer to God, in the name of His Church, to restrain this diabolical power supernaturally, and a profession of faith in His willingness to do so on behalf of His servants on earth.*

The most interesting thing I find in this is that the Catholic Church considers exorcism *"nothing more than a prayer to God, in the name of His Church"* and that demons are cast out *"in the name of God, or any of the higher powers in which he is subject."*

---

1    The Catholic Encyclopedia. New York: Robert Appleton Company. (1909)

The Bible, according to Catholicism, is the inspired word of God, yet their scholars have missed a key theme throughout the New Testament. 'In the name of the church' is never mentioned nor is any 'higher powers' other than the name of Jesus. Jesus Himself said:

*And whatsoever ye shall ask in my name, that will I do, that the Father may be glorified in the Son.*

John 14:13

*And these signs shall accompany them that believe: in my name shall they cast out demons;...*

Mark 16:17

*And the seventy returned with joy, saying, Lord, even the demons are subject unto us in thy (Jesus) name.*

Luke 10:17

Notice that according to the Bible, which the Catholic Church believes to be God's word, it is in the name of Jesus that demons are cast out, NOT in the name of the Catholic Church.

A House Blessing and House Cleansing/Exorcism are two separate rituals. To have a house blessed is as easy as asking a priest to come bless your home. The Priest will usually move from room to room, sprinkling Holy Water and reciting either the Lord's Prayer (Our Father) or a chant in Latin.

To have a house cleansed or exorcised is typically a long and usually difficult process. Once someone decides that his home has something living in it, besides his family, he or she will usually talk to a priest. The official doctrine of the Catholic Church is to ignore it. "If you ignore it, it will go away." Several weeks later it's back to the priest, oftentimes the situation has gotten worse. The priest will contact the Diocese and get permission to investigate. Again, this takes time. If permission is granted, a priest will be appointed to visit the home. If that priest finds evidence of a haunting he will contact the Diocese again and request permission for an exorcism, again taking more time. If the Diocese determines an exorcism is necessary, a priest who is schooled in the rituals of exorcism will be sent to perform an exorcism. It may take a year or more to get to this point.

On November 12, 2010 CBS News ran this headline:

## Exorcism Training Offered By Catholic Bishops

### 2-Day Conference Instructs Clergy on Evaluating Whether Person is Truly Possessed and Reviews Prayers that Comprise Rite

(AP) **Citing a shortage of priests who can perform the rite, the nation's Roman Catholic bishops are sponsoring a conference on how to conduct exorcisms.**

The article goes on to give details of the classes that are centered on the exorcism of people, not places. However, the process of determining if an exorcism is needed is the same and just as lengthy. Apparently the Catholic Church, whose official doctrine is to 'ignore it and it will go away.' realizes there is a need for serious spiritual warfare in this world of ours. More than 50 bishops and 60 priests signed up to attend the class.

An old friend of my family and a good friend of my dad's is a Roman Catholic priest. He and I had an interesting discussion prior to my writing this book. I asked him about Catholic exorcism ceremonies. He told me that he had been involved in several house blessings and a few house cleansings/exorcisms and that in no uncertain terms "I will never do it again!" Several times when he would go into homes to bless them strange things would happen. He would see black masses, things would move and he would hear strange noises. During a few exorcisms of people he had been involved with things just got "weird" and he had been spat on many times and vomited on more than once. During the exorcism of a house things had been thrown at him by entities no one could see. He explained that even after the blessings and cleansing, whatever was there oftentimes wouldn't leave or would come back later.

Having entities remain after a Catholic Blessing or Cleansing is not uncommon. Sometimes it seems that whatever was in the house will leave for a while, a month, a year or more. If it comes back, it usually comes back with a vengeance. There have been many families driven from their homes by things they couldn't see after a priest has performed a ritual exorcism.

## Praying The Rosary, Chants And Mantras

According to tradition, the rosary was given to Saint Dominic in an apparition by the Blessed Virgin Mary in the year 1214 in the church of Prouille. Rosary beads are typically held in the hands as a person prays and a bead is moved between the fingers at the end of a prayer. These prayers are repeated until all the beads have been passed through the fingers. However, rosary beads or prayer beads have been around far longer than the Catholic Church.

The earliest use of prayer beads can be traced to Hinduism about 900BC, where they are called Japa Mala. Japa is the repeating of the name of a deity or a mantra (a prayer). *Mala* means "garland" or "wreath". Japa mala are used for repetition of a mantra and as an aid to meditation. Hinduism regards many different gods and which god or gods a person reveres most will determine the mantra(s) used.

Within witchcraft, the use of the rosary prayer beads can add a certain tactile element not often found in most chanted prayers. There is a long history of their use in pagan and satanic culture. In Southern Italy, witches have long used prayer beads to break spells and heal impotency.

A *chant* is the rhythmic speaking or singing of words or sounds offered as a prayer, often primarily using one or two pitches called *reciting tones*. Chanting a mantra, sacred text, the name of a god or a spirit is a commonly used spiritual practice found in many New Age religions, Wicca and witchcraft. Like prayer, chanting may be a component of either personal or group practice.

For many people with a ghost/demon in the home, the first line of defense tends to be praying the rosary. Very few find any relief by doing so. What typically happens is that the demon gets agitated and makes things worse. Most Catholics are taught that God will listen to them if they pray the Lord's Prayer (Our Father) and the Hail Mary enough times. However, Christ Jesus Himself said:

> But when ye pray, use not vain repetitions, as the heathen do: for they think that they shall be heard for their much speaking.
>
> Matthew 6:7

From this verse we can determine that Jesus, apparently, never prayed the Rosary and saying the same prayer over and over doesn't interest God. There comes a point when a person is repeating the same thing over and over that his heart and mind is no longer in it. After the prayer, chant or mantra has been said just a few times the subconscious and the mouth are capable of continuing on while the conscious mind wanders off onto something else. The fact is, repeating the same prayer does very little when trying to remove a ghost and often does more harm than good.

## Sage Burning

The use of sage springs from at least two powerful spiritual, ancient sources. The ancient Celts, including the Druids, and the Native Americans have used sage for many purposes. Some of these include using sage as an anti-convulsant, to staunch bleeding and as a stimulant. It was commonly used as a purifying smoke smudge and as a poultice for festering sores and wounds and as a tea.

Today, sage burning ceremonies are commonly done within New Age Religions, Wicca and witchcraft. Burning it slowly as a smudge and wafting its smoke in the air throughout one's home is an example of a cleansing ritual to establish positive energy, clear thinking, healing and supposedly removing ghosts. However, I have known a few people, including a very close relative, who have performed sage burning ceremonies to remove ghosts from their homes and nothing happened other than making the house smell like a campground.

However, this isn't to say that it hasn't worked in some instances. There have been many reports of ghosts being removed or appeased by sage ceremonies. This can be verified by the many television documentaries and books on the subject. In most cases it turned out to be just a temporary fix.

## Anointing With Holy Water And Blessed Oil

In Christianity, oil and water are two of the symbols of the Holy Spirit. Using these for anointing is a common practice for the purpose of blessing a person, place or object. Wikipedia defines anointing as:

> To pour or smear with oil, milk, water, melted butter or other substances, a process employed ritually by many religions. People and things are anointed to symbolize the introduction of a sacramental or divine influence, a holy emanation, spirit, power or god. It can also be seen as a spiritual mode of ridding persons and things of dangerous influences, as of demons believed to be or to cause disease.

There are different methods to anoint someone or something depending on the purpose and what medium is being used. In the Old Testament it was common practice to pour olive oil over the head of a newly crowned king or newly appointed priests

> Then shalt thou take the anointing oil, and pour it upon his head, and anoint him.
>
> *Exodus 29:7*

Since that time, using a finger to wipe holy water or blessed oil (water or oil blessed by a priest or pastor) on a person's forehead or onto an object such as the top post of a door frame has become common practice, often in the sign of a cross. Within the Catholic Church and a few other denominations it is common to see holy water sprinkled using an *aspergill* or *aspergillum*. This is a brush or branch used to sprinkle the water. Often thought to be a Catholic ritual, this has been a practice among some Orthodox Jews since the time of Moses.

*And a clean person shall take hyssop, and dip it in the water, and sprinkle it upon the tent, and upon all the vessels, and upon the persons that were there,*

*Numbers 19:18*

In the New Testament, Jesus speaks about living water flowing from those who believe on Him. The Apostle John explains that Jesus was using water as a symbol of the Holy Spirit.

*Now on the last day, the great day of the feast, Jesus stood and cried, saying, If any man thirst, let him come unto me and drink. He that believeth on me, as the scripture hath said, from within him shall flow rivers of living water. But this spake he of the Spirit, which they that believed on him were to receive: for the Spirit was not yet given; because Jesus was not yet glorified.*

*John 7:37-39*

Like praying the rosary, anointing a home with holy water or blessed oil to dispel ghosts and demons is a common practice, often performed together. Many believe this is a 'sure-fire' remedy for unseen entities since the water or oil has been blessed. holy water and blessed oil have no power in and of themselves. They are simply a symbol of the Holy Spirit and are a sign of His presence.

*Is any among you sick? Let him call for the elders of the church; and let them pray over him, anointing him with oil in the name of the Lord:*

*James 5:14*

In this scripture the elders of churches are appointed to pray for and anoint those who are sick. However the prayers and anointing must be done in the name of the Lord (Jesus). The term *'In the name of*' is an ancient way of saying '*to the glory of*' or '*in the power of*' an authority of some form. How many movies have we seen where a knight comes to a person or group and tells them "I come in the name of the king!"? That knight is telling them that he "comes in the power, authority and for the glory of" the king he represents. When a ghost/demon is commanded to leave a person, place or thing it must be done with the power and for the glory of our Lord Jesus.

*Verily, verily, I say unto you, He that believeth on me, the works that I do shall he do also; and greater works than these shall he do; because I go unto my Father. And whatsoever ye shall ask in my name, that will I do, that the Father may be glorified in the Son*

*John 14:12-13*

*... Verily, verily, I say unto you, Whatsoever ye shall ask the Father in my name, he will give it you.*

*John 16:23*

Why then are there times when we pray for something, like for a ghost to leave, that God doesn't honor our prayers and the entity won't leave? Often, people will pray and end the prayer saying "in the name of the Father and the Son and the Holy Spirit" and the entity still will not leave. Oftentimes the problem is that there is sin in the person's life for which they have not asked forgiveness. This will be discussed later in this book. If the problem isn't sin in a person's life then it may be that the person trying to cast out the ghost is doing it for his own reasons and not for God's glory. The person may want recognition, money or some other selfish reason.

*Ye ask, and receive not, because ye ask amiss, that ye may consume it upon your lusts.*

*James 4:3*

Why use oil or water to anoint someone or something if it doesn't have any actual power over ghosts? Since we know from scripture that it's through the name of Jesus ghosts are cast out, there must be a reason for anointing with holy water and blessed oil.

> And the blood shall be to you for a token upon the houses where ye are: and when I see the blood, I will pass over you, and the plague shall not be upon you to destroy you, when I smite the land of Egypt.
>
> *Exodus 12:13*

> And ye shall take a bunch of hyssop, and dip it in the blood that is in the bason, and strike the lintel and the two side posts with the blood that is in the bason; and none of you shall go out at the door of his house until the morning. For the LORD will pass through to smite the Egyptians; and when he seeth the blood upon the lintel, and on the two side posts, the LORD will pass over the door, and will not suffer the destroyer to come in unto your houses to smite you.
>
> *Exodus 12:22*

Because Jesus was the final sacrifice for humanity, blood is no longer used for anointing in Christianity. However, it is still used in other religions that don't recognize the sacrifice Jesus made. Before Jesus' blood was shed on the cross, Moses was instructed by God to have all of the Israelites use a branch of hyssop to sprinkle lambs' blood on the lintel (top post) and the two side posts of their doors as a token (sign or symbol) so the destroyer would not enter their homes. The blood was a symbol of ownership. Sprinkling or smearing water or oil is also a symbol of ownership letting all spirits, both heavenly and demonic know who the owner is.

## Crosses And Crucifixes

Quite often when someone realizes he has an entity living in his home he will hang crosses or crucifixes on the walls. Once in a while I will hear of someone who did so and the next morning or when they came home from work the crosses or crucifixes were turned upside down, bent and twisted, laying on the floor or thrown across the room. Demons don't like crosses and crucifixes because of what they represent. However, like holy water and blessed oil, crosses and crucifixes have no power in and of themselves. They are symbols of an all loving God Who sacrificed Himself to save us from hell.

*and being found in fashion as a man, he humbled himself, becoming obedient even unto death, yea, the death of the cross.*

*Philippians 2:8*

*and through him to reconcile all things unto himself, having made peace through the blood of his cross; through him, I say, whether things upon the earth, or things in the heavens. And you, being in time past alienated and enemies in your mind in your evil works, yet now hath he reconciled in the body of his flesh through death, to present you holy and without blemish and unreproveable before him:*

*Colossians 1:20-22*

To demons crosses and crucifixes are reminders of the destruction they eventually face as a result of Jesus' death on the cross.

*And in the synagogue there was a man, that had a spirit of an unclean demon; and he cried out with a loud voice, Ah! what have we to do with thee, Jesus thou Nazarene?* **art thou come to destroy us?** *I know thee who thou art, the Holy One of God. (emphasis added)*

*Luke 4:33-34*

*And the devil that deceived them was cast into the lake of fire and brimstone, where the beast and the false prophet are, and shall be tormented day and night for ever and ever.*

*Revelation 20:10*

*Then shall he say also unto them on the left hand, Depart from me, ye cursed, into everlasting fire, prepared for the devil and his angels:*

*Matthew 25:41*

The fact is that most people put crosses and crucifixes on their walls or hang them around their necks as good luck charms. They believe that by doing so God will protect them regardless of what they believe or how they live their lives. The Cross is not so much a piece of wood as it is the act of Jesus sacrificing Himself for us and when Satan and his armies were defeated. Their destruction is imminent and they don't like being reminded of that fact by looking at crosses and crucifixes.

## Quoting Scripture

Quite often when someone has a ghost in his home he will quote verses from the Bible, even those who don't believe in the Bible have been known to do this. Many are under the impression that Satan and demons can't stand to hear scripture quoted and will run as fast as they can to get away. If only this were true. The fact is that Satan and his fallen angels know the Bible better than any human. After all, they've had thousands of years to get to know it and they have far better memories than we do. Satan quoted scripture from memory when he was trying to tempt Jesus in Matthew Chapter 4.

> Then the devil taketh him into the holy city; and he set him on the pinnacle of the temple, and saith unto him, If thou art the Son of God, cast thyself down: for it is written, He shall give his angels charge concerning thee: and, On their hands they shall bear thee up, Lest haply thou dash thy foot against a stone.
>
> *Matthew 4:5-6*

But just because Satan and his minions know the Bible doesn't mean we shouldn't quote it.

> For no word from God shall be void of power.
>
> *Luke 1:37*

> For the kingdom of God is not in word, but in power.
>
> *1Corinthians 4:20*

Speaking the Word of God has power because the Word of God IS power. For those who do not know Jesus as their Lord or those who do, but have sin in their lives, the power in the Word of God can be hindered.

*Behold, the Lord's hand is not shortened, that it cannot save; neither his ear heavy, that it cannot hear: but your iniquities have separated between you and your God, and your sins have hid his face from you, that he will not hear.*

Isaiah 59:1,2.

*For the eyes of the Lord are over the righteous, and his ears are open unto their prayers: but the face of the Lord is against them that do evil.*

I Peter 3:12.

*If I regard iniquity in my heart, the Lord will not hear me.*

Psalm 66:18.

# CHAPTER 5

~

## Who Can Get Rid Of Ghosts?

## Pastors And Priests

In the section on rituals, I talked a bit about why many priests have difficulty casting out ghosts. However, the problem often goes deeper than just repetitive prayers and ancient rituals. I have known both priests and pastors who can give great sermons, but in getting to know the person behind the robes I've learned something disturbing; not all pastors and priests believe in the sacrifice Jesus made for us and therefore are unable to draw on the power God has made available to cast out demons. Just because someone is a pastor or priest doesn't mean he believes what he teaches.

When I was in school, one of my professors told a story about the pastor of a church he had attended. One Sunday morning the pastor was giving a wonderful sermon on salvation through the death and resurrection of Jesus. Toward the end of the sermon, the pastor suddenly dropped to his knees in front of the congregation and accepted Jesus as his savior. As my professor said, "The pastor got saved!"

> And these signs shall follow **them that believe;** In my name shall they cast out devils; they shall speak with new tongues; They shall take up serpents; and if they drink any deadly thing, it shall not hurt them; they shall lay hands on the sick, and they shall recover. (Emphasis added)
>
> Mark 16:17-18

> But as many as received him, to them gave he power to become the sons of God, even to **them that believe** on his name: (Emphasis added)
>
> John 1:12

*For God so loved the world, that he gave his only begotten Son, that **whosoever believeth** in him should not perish, but have everlasting life. (Emphasis added)*

*John 3:16*

According to Strongs Concordance of the Bible, the Greek word for *believe* in these verses is *pisteuō*. It defines this word as *to think to be true, to be persuaded of, to credit, place confidence in*. This doesn't mean to just believe in the existence of God, but rather to trust in, rely on and cling to Him no matter what may happen. Just because someone believes in the existence of God doesn't mean he is saved or going to heaven, much less has any power over ghosts, regardless of his position within a church. In the book of Job, Satan and God had a conversation so, obviously, Satan believes God exists. The demons know God and who Jesus is, but they know Him not as their savior, but as their judge and eventual destroyer.

*Now there was a day when the sons of God came to present themselves before the LORD, and Satan came also among them. And the LORD said unto Satan, Whence comest thou? Then Satan answered the LORD, and said, From going to and fro in the earth, and from walking up and down in it.*

*Job 1:6-7*

*And straightway there was in their synagogue a man with an unclean spirit; and he cried out, saying, What have we to do with thee, Jesus thou Nazarene? art thou come to destroy us? I know thee who thou art, the Holy One of God.*

*Mark 1:23-24*

*Thou believest that there is one God; thou doest well: the devils also believe, and tremble.*

*James 2:19*

Many people, including pastors and priests, are religious, looking and doing the things that make them appear to be pious and 'Christian' but do not have a relationship with the Lord. God isn't interested in religion. The power God has given us 'in the name of Jesus' comes from our relationship with Him and not the religious things we do. Since the time of Adam, God has wanted a relationship with humanity.

*I will be his father, and he shall be my son.*

*2Samual 7:14*

*And the scripture was fulfilled which saith,* **Abraham believed God**, *and it was imputed unto him for righteousness: and he was called the* **Friend of God.** *(Emphasis added)*

*James 2:23*

If you are going to ask a pastor or priest to come cast out a ghost, find out if they have a relationship or just a religion with God.

## Mediums And Shaman

[1]**Mediumship** is " *a form of communication with spirits. It is a practice in religious beliefs such as Spiritualism, Spiritism, Espiritismo, Candomblé, Louisiana Voodoo, Shambala and Umbanda.*"

[2] **Shamanism** is *"an anthropological term referencing a range of beliefs and practices regarding communication with the spiritual world within undeveloped tribes."*

By these definitions from Wikipedia it can be said that mediums and shaman are, for all practical purposes, the same thing, mediums being 'modern' and shaman being 'tribal'. During this chapter I will use the term medium to refer to both mediums and shaman. Since both communicate with spirits the question becomes, which spirits? Both angels and demons are spirits.

 The most common way for mediums to connect to the spirit world is through 'channeling'. Channeling is a form of divination used in receiving messages or inspiration from invisible beings or spirits. In doing so, a *spirit guide,* also called a *familiar spirit,* is used as a go-between from the medium and the spirit world. A spirit guide is a highly evolved spirit with the sole purpose of helping the medium develop and use personal skills. Mediums claim the spirits assist in the person's following a spiritual path. Other mediums claim a spirit guide is one who brings other spirits to a medium's attention or carries communications between a medium and the spirits of the dead. Contact with these spirits is initiated by a medium.

> … And the angel of Jehovah called unto him out of heaven, and said, Abraham, Abraham. And he said, Here I am.
>
> *Genesis 22:10-11*

*And the angel of Jehovah appeared unto him, and said unto him, Jehovah is with thee, thou mighty man of valor.*

*Judges 6:12*

*And the angel of Jehovah appeared unto the woman, and said unto her, Behold now, thou art barren, and bearest not; but thou shalt conceive, and bear a son.*

*Judge 13:3*

*He saw in a vision openly, as it were about the ninth hour of the day, an angel of God coming in unto him, and saying to him,...*

*Act 10:3*

Nowhere in the Bible is communication with angels initiated by mediums or any other human. Any time someone has spoken with an angel of God the conversation was initiated by the angel as sent by God and there is no 'middle-man' such as a medium or spirit guide. If an angel is sent to talk with someone, he speaks with that person directly.

*For these nations, that thou shalt dispossess, hearken unto them that practise augury, and unto diviners; but as for thee, Jehovah thy God hath not suffered thee so to do.*

*Deuteronomy 18:14*

We see in this verse that God commands Israel and us, as His children, not to be involved in augury (to interpret the will of the gods by studying the flight of birds **and other 'omens'**) or divination (speaking to spirits.)

In the 28th Chapter of 1 Samuel, Saul, the King of Israel, consorted with a medium. In so doing, the deceased prophet, Samuel, appeared before them to condemn Saul. As a result of Saul's discussion with the dead, his kingdom was taken from him and the nation of Israel was taken captive.

*And inasmuch as it is appointed unto men once to die, and after this cometh judgment;*

*Hebrews 9:27*

It's not the spirits of the dead that mediums speak with, but rather the spirits that seek to deceive. Although there have been many times when mediums have helped police departments solve crimes, there have been many more cases in which the medium was given false information or 'made up' information which actually hindered investigations.

When famous modern day mediums like John Edward, Sylvia Browne or some other medium can't get a good 'reading' on a person or an audience, they say that sometimes the messages come in bits and pieces, sometimes they don't understand what they see or sometimes they misinterpret the information they were given. If they're wrong it's not their fault since they never claimed to be perfect. Sylvia Browne, seen many times on the Montel Williams Show, claims to have about an 85% accuracy rate. Ryan Shaffer and Agatha Jadwiszczok in 2010, investigated 115 criminal cases that Browne worked on and state that her accuracy rate is in reality "zero!" Sylvia's biography on Wikipedia makes for interesting reading concerning her abilities as a medium and many of her predictions.

The fact is that even the best mediums that write for magazines and periodicals have an accuracy rate of 85% or less. The spirits that mediums communicate with will give enough accurate information often enough to make a medium sound legitimate. Usually most information and prophesies they claim to get from their spirit guides are so generalized they would fit a variety of people, situations or are outright inaccurate. This is very true of Nostradamus as well. Living in Southern California we get a lot of prophesies from mediums about when, where and the severity of earthquakes going to happen here. Of course one or two will get it right eventually; after all, this is the American Earthquake Capitol.

> But the prophet, that shall speak a word presumptuously in my name, which I have not commanded him to speak, or that shall speak in the name of other gods, that same prophet shall die. And if thou say in thy heart, How shall we know the word which Jehovah hath not spoken? when a prophet speaketh in the name of Jehovah, if the thing follow not, nor come to pass, that is the thing which Jehovah hath not spoken: the prophet hath spoken it presumptuously, thou shalt not be afraid of him.
>
> *Deuteronomy 18:20-22*

A true prophet of God has a 100% accuracy rate! Anything less means that person is not speaking from God. He is speaking from his own mind or from a lying spirit. A spirit who lies cannot be from God, but is sent from the father of lies, Satan. Also, any word given from God will not come in bits and pieces, but rather ALL pertinent information is given with total clarity and understanding.

## Paranormal Groups

There is a large number of "paranormal research" groups out there. Most of them have little or nothing to do with actually trying to remove ghosts. The majority of these groups are amateur 'ghost hunters' looking for the thrill of what they may find. Most carry with them various kinds of cameras and recording devices hoping to catch something on film, tape or digital format. When confronted with demonic activity in a home they refer the homeowner to some other group, quite often the Catholic Church, mediums and members of Wicca covens to remove the ghosts.

Many paranormal groups, like one based not far from where I live, are actually covers for Witch and Wicca covens. An acquaintance of mine had joined a paranormal group near me not knowing it was a guise for a coven. Like most, she was hoping to go out and get photos and recordings of unseen entities. This group would often visit local cemeteries and known haunted locations looking for ghosts. She soon found herself watching satanic rituals being performed that involved animal blood sacrifices and the calling up of different demons for worship.

## Christians

First of all, what is a Christian? Most churches, and the people that attend them, claim to be 'Christian'. However, when we compare what many churches and people believe and teach, we find that their definition of Christianity is different than that of the Bible. Just because someone warms a pew every Sunday doesn't make him a Christian, nor does wearing robes, being baptized, performing religious rites or any other form of work for the Lord. These things make a person 'religious'.

> for by grace have ye been saved through faith; and that not of yourselves, it is the gift of God; not of works, that no man should boast.
>
> *Ephesians 2:8*

> not by works done in righteousness, which we did ourselves, but according to his mercy he saved us, through the washing of regeneration and renewing of the Holy Spirit,
>
> *Titus 3:5*

> And the scripture was fulfilled which saith, Abraham believed God, and it was imputed unto him for righteousness: and he was called the Friend of God.
>
> *James 2:23*

> Behold, what manner of love the Father hath bestowed upon us, that we should be called the sons of God
>
> *1John 3:1*

A true Christian is a person who has a relationship with God, as a person has with his best friend. I've known my best friend for over forty years. He and I have always been able to rely on each other regardless of the situation. I love him as my own brother. I don't have to put on special cloths or robes when I go see him and I don't have to perform any special rituals or get on my knees and close my eyes when I talk with him. There isn't a topic under the sun we can't talk about with each other. If I do something to make him mad at me, I go to him and take care of it to restore that friendship. THIS is the kind of relationship God wants with us.

> *For since by man came death, by man came also the resurrection of the dead. For as in Adam all die, even so in Christ shall all be made alive.*
>
> *1Corinthians 15:21*

Because Adam, a perfect man, brought sin into the world causing spiritual death and the loss of relationship with God, it took the sacrifice of a perfect man, Jesus, to take the place in our death sentence, remove that sin, and to restore that relationship. All He asks is to admit that we have sinned and become His friend.

> *That if thou shalt confess with thy mouth the Lord Jesus, and shalt believe in thine heart that God hath raised him from the dead, thou shalt be saved*
>
> *Romans 10:9*

> *If we confess our sins, he is faithful and just to forgive us our sins, and to cleanse us from all unrighteousness.*
>
> *1John 1:9*

> *Whosoever shall confess that Jesus is the Son of God, God dwelleth in him, and he in God.*
>
> *1John 4:15*

There are many people in various countries who are unable to attend a church or have any outward form of Christianity in public for fear of imprisonment or even death. Even though they are unable to perform any formal rituals they love the Lord and call Him their friend.

## Powers Over Ghosts Given To Christians By God

*Wherefore thou art no more a servant, but a son; and if a son, then an heir of God through Christ.*

*Galatians 4:7*

At the time of the writing of the New Testament, Israel was under Roman law. According to the laws of the times, when a child was adopted he had the same rights as a natural born child, including equal authority and inheritance from the parents.

*But as many as received him, to them gave he power to become the sons of God, even to them that believe on his name:*

*John 1:12*

*For ye received not the spirit of bondage again unto fear; but ye received the spirit of adoption, whereby we cry, Abba, Father.*

*Romans 8:15*

Although we have God as our Father by adoption, He dare not grant us all of the rights and power given to his natural Son, Jesus, for our own good. Some of the things not allowed being that we are not, nor will we ever be gods and that Jesus, being God, can forgive sin and we cannot. Nor can we create life, as God did.

*But that ye may know that the Son of man hath authority on earth to forgive sins (then saith he to the sick of the palsy), Arise, and take up thy bed, and go up unto thy house.*

*Matthew 9:6*

*And Jesus seeing their faith saith unto the sick of the palsy, Son, thy sins are forgiven. But there were certain of the scribes sitting there, and reasoning in their hearts, Why doth this man thus speak? he blasphemeth: who can forgive sins but one, even God?*

*Mark 2:5-7*

But, of the rights God has granted us, He also granted us the power to use those rights.

> And these signs shall accompany them that believe: in my name shall they cast out demons; they shall speak with new tongues; They shall take up serpents; and if they drink any deadly thing, it shall not hurt them; they shall lay hands on the sick, and they shall recover.
>
> *Mark 16:17 -18*

Just as Jesus commanded demons to leave, we have been given that authority through our belief. Remember the definition of belief here is not just to believe in the existence of God, but rather to trust and rely on His authority. It's not always a simple thing to force a ghost to leave. Many are reluctant to go. There are typically three reasons a ghost may not leave when commanded to do so by a true Christian.

The first we have already discussed, sin in a persons life. The second reason is lack of faith. For a Christian that has never experienced some of the things that can happen when removing ghosts from a home, it can be rather unnerving and frightening. This can lead to a lack of trust that God will both protect those in attendance from harm and actually force the entity to leave. People who first meet are not best friends, trusting each other instantly. It takes time to get to know each other and learn to trust each other. It's the same with our relationship with God. As we get to know Him more and more we begin to trust Him more and more. As our relationship with God matures we will learn to trust Him in all things, even dealing with reluctant to leave demons.

The third reason is that some demons have great power in comparison to others. A demon of lower rank and little authority will usually be easier to cast out than one of very high rank and with great power. Regardless of a demons' power, he is still subject to the authority given Christians 'in the name of Jesus'. Some demons can be of such great power that preparation must be made before attempting to command them, and those with them, to leave. I'll talk more about this later.

> *Lord, have mercy on my son: for he is epileptic, and suffereth grievously; for oft-times he falleth into the fire, and off-times into the water. And I brought him to thy disciples, and they could not cure him. And Jesus answered and said, O faithless and perverse generation, how long shall I be with you? how long shall I bear with you? bring him hither to me. And Jesus rebuked him; and the demon went out of him: and the boy was cured from that hour. Then came the disciples to Jesus apart, and said, Why could not we cast it out? And he saith unto them, Because of your little faith: for verily I say unto you, If ye have faith as a grain of mustard seed, ye shall say unto this mountain, Remove hence to yonder place; and it shall remove; and nothing shall be impossible unto you. But this kind goeth not out save by prayer and fasting.*

> *Matthew 17:15-21*

> *Know ye not that we shall judge angels?*

> *1Corinthians 6:3*

If we are to judge angels, both heavenly (to their glory) and fallen (to their destruction) then we, as children of God, must be of higher authority than those angels. Understanding this is imperative to making a ghost leave.

# CHAPTER 6

*Getting Rid Of Ghosts*

To those reading this book who do not have a relationship with Jesus, please do not attempt to cast out a ghost on your own. Without the power and authority given by God to his children, the best you can hope for is to get the ghost to leave temporarily. A few days or possibly months later they will likely come back and usually with a vengeance. Contact the pastor of a church who teaches relationship and not religion and who knows the power he has through Jesus.

To those that know Jesus as their savior, this next chapter is more for you than those asking for your help. I don't have a set ritual when I go to cast out ghosts. You already know how I feel about rituals. I ask for guidance and allow the Lord to lead because each exorcism is different. If He gives me or someone in the group inspiration, we go with the flow of God's Holy Spirit.

## Talking To Those Living In The Home

The first part of the process to cleansing a home is to interview the people that live there. Some of the things you will want to know are:

### Are they Christians? If not, what do they believe?

I've found that if the people living in the home are Christians, even if they accept Jesus as their savior or renew their faith during the interview process, it is easier to remove a ghost if all are God's children and in agreement. If the family is not Christian, the demons can still be made to leave, but it is imperative to take precautions so that they will not return. Keeping ghosts/demons from returning will be discussed later.

## What has been happening in the home? Ask them to be as specific as possible.

Does the haunting seem to be 'weird' feelings, unexplained footsteps, things moving by themselves, strange knockings or noises, etc? Has the entity touched or hurt anyone? Do they know the history of the home, especially relating to accidents, murders, satanic practices, etc. that has taken place in the home. Typically, the more power the demon has, the more severe the haunting.

## What does the Lord impress on you?

Before entering a home, I pray. I ask the Lord to let me know what's going on as I enter each room. In one home, as I went from room to room, God impressed on me that there had been witchcraft practiced in two of the bedrooms. When I asked about it I was told that the couple's daughter used to read tarot cards and very likely used a Ouija Board in those rooms. It was also impressed upon me that there had been drug use and pre-marital sex in some of the rooms. They told me they were sure two of their children had done so.

I went to visit a friend one evening for dinner. During the course of the evening I kept getting the impression of a demon of depression coming from one end of the house. My friend told me that his roommate had lost his job and was severely depressed. We talked about praying with him at some time when he was home. We never got the chance to pray together, but the demon left when the roommate moved out.

## Could there be natural explanations for all or some of the things happening in the home?

There are some ghost hunting groups that try to disprove hauntings. In doing so, they try to find natural reasons for odd noises, feelings and other things thought to be paranormal. Quite often, especially in older homes, they find loose plumbing that bangs against walls and beams that can sound like footsteps and knocking sounds. Most ghost hunting groups use Electro-Magnetic Frequency (EMF) meters to check for high readings of electro-magnetic energy coming from components of electrical systems. High EMF readings can lead to odd feelings, feelings of nausea and feelings of being watched. I'm not saying you need equipment like this, but there are times it can come in handy when looking for natural causes of odd feelings.

# Preparation For Battle

## The Armor of God

Put on the whole armor of God, that ye may be able to stand against the wiles of the devil. For our wrestling is not against flesh and blood, but against the principalities, against the powers, against the world-rulers of this darkness, against the spiritual hosts of wickedness in the heavenly places. Wherefore take up the whole armor of God, that ye may be able to withstand in the evil day, and, having done all, to stand. Stand therefore, having girded your loins with truth, and having put on the breastplate of righteousness, and having shod your feet with the preparation of the gospel of peace; withal taking up the shield of faith, wherewith ye shall be able to quench all the fiery darts of the evil one. And take the helmet of salvation, and the sword of the Spirit, which is the word of God:

*Ephesians 6:11-17*

As the Apostle Paul was writing this he was imprisoned in Rome awaiting his trial for his belief in Jesus. During this time he was constantly guarded by members of the Roman army. He relates the description of their armor to the attributes needed for spiritual warfare. Paul describes in verses 11 and 12 very real, intense, vicious warfare, even though we don't see it with our eyes.

**Gird your loins with truth**- When dressing for spiritual warfare, the first thing we want to put on is truth. Truth in our lives, which includes our personal sincerity and integrity, as well as the truth that Jesus is who He said He is.

*And they that were in the boat worshipped him, saying, Of a truth thou art the Son of God.*

*Matthew 14:33*

**Put on the breastplate of righteousness-** This bronze plate covers both the chest and the stomach area, protecting the vital organs. By living our lives in a pure, righteous manner we give no place for Satan and his demons to attack our personal lives.

*But the salvation of the righteous is of Jehovah; He is their stronghold in the time of trouble.*

*Psalm 37:39*

**Shod your feet with the preparation of the gospel of peace-** Shoes are made for walking, not just for wearing as we take up space in a pew. Jesus commands us to get out and spread His Word so the whole world will hear. By doing so we not only build our own faith but we open heaven to others.

*And he said unto them, Go ye into all the world, and preach the gospel to the whole creation.*

*Mark 16:15*

**Taking up the shield of faith, wherewith ye shall be able to quench all the fiery darts of the evil one-** Faith, trusting in God, is that which we hold out in front of us when times get hard. No matter what Satan throws at us, God will be there for us and all we have to do is trust Him.

*And my God shall supply every need of yours according to his riches in glory in Christ Jesus.*

*Philippians 4:19*

**And take up the helmet of salvation**- Notice that it doesn't say 'earn the helmet of salvation'. Salvation cannot be earned; it is a gift that God has given us that we do not deserve. The knowledge that we truly are saved from God's judgment is a reason for rejoicing to us and protection from the lies with which Satan and demons will try to infect our minds.

> *But I have trusted in thy lovingkindness; My heart shall rejoice in thy salvation.*
>
> *Psalm 13:5*

> *O Jehovah the Lord, the strength of my salvation, Thou hast covered my head in the day of battle.*
>
> *Psalm 140:7*

**Sword of the Spirit, which is the word of God**- This is the only offensive weapon Paul mentions. In the hands of a trained soldier it is a devastating and deadly weapon. Memorizing and quoting scriptures from the Bible is like putting a sharp blade of truth and promises from God into the face of our enemy. When Satan and the fallen angels bring trouble, either in our personal lives or when removing them from a home, reminding them that God has given His adopted children irrevocable promises such as salvation and authority over them, give them no choice but to comply.

> *Let the high praises of God be in their mouth, And a two-edged sword in their hand;*
>
> *Psalm 149:6*

> *For the word of God is living, and active, and sharper than any two-edged sword, and piercing even to the dividing of soul and spirit, of both joints and marrow, and quick to discern the thoughts and intents of the heart.*
>
> *Hebrews 4:12*

**Note:** There is no armor for the back. We are never to turn our backs on the enemy. If we do, they will take every advantage to spear our emotions, our spirits and to drag us as far from God as they can.

## Prayer And Prayer Groups

Prior to going into a home to confront the ghosts, there are certain things that should be done. The most important is prayer! If, after interviewing the residents, you feel the demons you may be dealing with could be powerful it is imperative to pray and fast, typically for 3 days prior to going into battle.

Ask the pastor to help you get a group of Christians together to pray. Generally I like to get a group together three or four days before I go into a home to get rid of ghosts, especially if I feel they may be of higher rank and having more power. I ask this group to come together again to pray for those of us going into the home the whole time we are confronting the spirits. Just prior to entering, the group going into the home prays together as well. It's amazing the amount of power prayer groups have.

When it comes to what to pray for, first pray for forgiveness of any sins you and those going into the home with you may have committed. By doing this we keep the conduit between us and the Lord open and unhindered.

*If we confess our sins, he is faithful and righteous to forgive us our sins, and to cleanse us from all unrighteousness*

*1John 1:9*

*Behold, the Lord's hand is not shortened, that it cannot save; neither his ear heavy, that it cannot hear: but your iniquities have separated between you and your God, and your sins have hid his face from you, that he will not hear.*

*Isaiah 59:1,2.*

*For the eyes of the Lord are over the righteous, and his ears are open unto their prayers: but the face of the Lord is against them that do evil.*

*I Peter 3:12.*

*If I regard iniquity in my heart, the Lord will not hear me.*

*Psalm 66:18.*

Next, ask for God's guidance. Ask Him to give you the words, scriptures, and any information you need about the ghosts such as their names or purpose. You may not receive anything until you actually need it, but it will come. It probably won't come as a voice from heaven, more likely you or someone will have an impression of something that happened, a word may suddenly pop into someone's head or someone who lives in the house may say something giving you the knowledge you need.

*for every one that asketh receiveth; and he that seeketh findeth; and to him that knocketh it shall be opened.*

*Matthew 7:8*

*But the Comforter, even the Holy Spirit, whom the Father will send in my name, he shall teach you all things, and bring to your remembrance all that I said unto you.*

*John 14:26*

*for I will give you a mouth and wisdom, which all your adversaries shall not be able to withstand or to gainsay.*

*Luke 21:15*

Very important is to ask for protection. This protection isn't just for our physical bodies, but our emotions and spirits as well. Whether you are dealing with demons of low rank or high they can get very upset and cause various things to happen. As part of this protection, ask the Lord to send angels as guardians of both your bodies and minds.

> *Thou wilt keep him in perfect peace, whose mind is stayed on thee;*
> *because he trusteth in thee.*

Isaiah 26: 3

> *Yea, thou I walk through the valley of the shadow of death, I will*
> *fear no evil; for thou art with me;*

Psalm 23:4

> *Behold, I* (Jesus) *have given you authority to tread upon serpents*
> *and scorpions* (Satan and demons), *and over all the power of*
> *the enemy: and nothing shall in any wise hurt you.* (Parenthesis
> added for clarity)

Luke 10:19

My father's friend, the Catholic priest, told me he had things thrown at him by unseen entities. He admitted that it scared him and this is why he will never be involved with anything like it again. I fear that he didn't ask for God's protection.


## Singing Praise Songs

As part of my preparation I like to have the group sing praise songs, songs that give glory to God and remind us who we are as God's children. During the few days between when the prayer group gets together and the time I go into the home I play a lot of praise CDs to keep my mind on the Lord.

## Fasting

Whether fasting can help rid the body of waste buildup is a matter of controversy. But fasting has been used for religious and spiritual purification for centuries. Nearly every religious text you can name, from the Old and New Testaments of the Bible to the Quran and the Upanishads, calls upon followers to fast periodically as a rite of spiritual purification, penitence, or preparation for union with God. Biblically, fasting is abstaining from food, drink, sleep or sex to focus on a period of spiritual growth. Specifically, we humbly deny something of the flesh to glorify God, enhance our spirit, and go deeper in our prayer life.

> Then came the disciples to Jesus apart, and said, Why could not we cast it out...(Jesus speaking) But this kind goeth not out save by prayer and fasting.
>
> Matthew 17:19, 21

When you fast, don't go all out and give up everything but water. It isn't healthy! Pick just one meal per day to begin with and rather than eating, spend that time in prayer. There are several good books on healthy ways to fast. A good website for information of Christian fasting is:

http://www.creatingfutures.net/fasting.htm

If you have fasted prior to going into spiritual battle with ghosts it is a good idea to have a good, high protein meal to restore your energy level a few hours before confronting the demons.

## Power In Numbers

When getting rid of a ghost, never do it alone. There is power in numbers. Always have at least one other person that is a Christian with you. There are a couple of reasons for this. First is that we want another Christian there for support. Should something happen, it's comforting to have another person in the room. Another great reason to have another Christian along is that Jesus tells us that He will be there with us.

> *Again I say unto you, that if two of you shall agree on earth as touching anything that they shall ask, it shall be done for them of my Father who is in heaven. For where two or three are gathered together in my name, there am I in the midst of them.*
>
> *Matthew 18:19-20*

> *Now after these things the Lord appointed seventy others, and sent them two and two before his face into every city and place, whither he himself was about to come.*
>
> *Luke 10:1*

## Letting The Ghosts Know Who You Are And Your Authority

When dealing with ghosts, it's an imperative to let them know who you are and by what authority you are there. After I have gone throughout the home, gathering and writing down the names or the positions of the entities the Lord impresses or gives to those in the group, I call out to any and all ghosts in that house and command them, in the name of Jesus, to listen to me. At this point you have their full attention. They have very good hearing and can hear me no matter where in the house they are. I tell them that I come by the authority of the owners of the house. Without the permission of the owners or occupants of the residence you really have no right to be there. Then I tell them that I come in the power and authority of Jesus Christ.

> *But certain also of the strolling Jews, exorcists, took upon them to name over them that had the evil spirits the name of the Lord Jesus, saying, I adjure you by Jesus whom Paul preacheth. And there were seven sons of one Sceva, a Jew, a chief priest, who did this. And the evil spirit answered and said unto them, Jesus I know, and Paul I know, but who are ye? And the man in whom the evil spirit was leaped on them, and mastered both of them, and prevailed against them, so that they fled out of that house naked and wounded.*
>
> *Acts 19:13-16*

Not only did the sons of Sceva not have a relationship with Jesus but, other than knowing that the Apostle Paul was preaching about Him, they didn't know who Jesus was! Once a person accepts Jesus as their savior the demons know it. Word gets around quickly in their ranks. Unless you have been adopted into God's family you have no power over demons and what happened to Sceva's sons has happened to others.

## Quoting Scripture

As I mentioned before, speaking the Word of God has power because the word of God IS power. Once I have the demons attention, and they know by what authority we are there, I will quote the scriptures proving our authority over them. I will tell them:

"I am a child of God through my faith in Jesus because God's Word says:"

> For ye are all sons of God, through faith, in Christ Jesus.
>
> Galatians 3:26

> For as many as are led by the Spirit of God, these are sons of God.
>
> Romans 8:14

> Behold what manner of love the Father hath bestowed upon us, that we should be called children of God; and such we are.
>
> 1John 3:1

"I have authority to bind you and to loose all the power of heaven upon you in Jesus' name by the power given to me in Matthew 18:18:"

> Verily I say unto you, what things soever ye shall bind on earth shall be bound in heaven; and what things soever ye shall loose on earth shall be loosed in heaven.
>
> Matthew 18:18

"I have the authority to cast you out of this place in Jesus' name by the authority given to me by Jesus words:"

> And these signs shall accompany them that believe: in my name shall they cast out demons;
>
> Mark 16:17

Proving authority over demons will make them realize that they have no authority over you. This may anger them or it may cause so much fear in them that they leave before you command them to leave.

More often than not, you will be dealing with more than one demon and one of those will usually be more powerful than the others. A term often used for the highest ranking demon is the *strongman*. The strongman will direct the others and force them to do his bidding. Sometimes there may be more than one strongman, each with demons associated with them. If a strongman is one of abuse, he may have underlings such as anger, perversion, malice, etc. in the home with him. If the strongman is witchcraft he may have demons of false religion, heresy, malice, denial or a host of other demons with him. God will give the names or purpose of the strongest demons if you ask for them. In all cases we have the authority to bind them together as stated in Matthew 18:18. By doing this, when we command the Strongman to leave, those associated with him must leave as well.

"In the name of Jesus, I bind the demon of abuse together with those associated with him and I command you all to leave this house in Jesus name!"

Demons like having a place to live. Once they have been displaced they want to find another place quickly. Since they were forcibly cast out they may hold a grudge and try to get revenge by attaching themselves to a person in the group and causing problems in his life or may follow him home, causing his house to be haunted, thankfully not so much with Christians. Once a home is 'clean,' and before you leave, everyone should pray together and ask the Lord to keep any of the demons removed from attaching themselves or following anyone home. Another thing to ask is for the Lord to place angels around the home to protect it from "re-infestation." More on this in a bit.

## Commanding Angels

Nowhere in the Bible does anyone but Jesus command angels. We have been given authority over fallen angels, not God's heavenly angels. However, we can ask God to send angels to protect us, comfort us, give us information or help in the fight against the demons we are dealing with.

> *Hast not thou made a hedge about him, and about his house, and about all that he hath, on every side? thou hast blessed the work of his hands, and his substance is increased in the land.*
>
> *Job 1:10*

The hedge talked about in Job 1:10 is a hedge of angels. These angels surround a person or a place to guard them. When we go into a home we pray together first. We ask for a hedge of angels to surround us and to protect us from any harm. One friend relates this as being surrounded by a very tall, invisible hedge of thorns so that no one, including demons, can get through or over.

In dealing with demons, I've known those who have had to ask the Lord for angels to restrain demons. In one case a demon was throwing things across a room trying to hurt someone. Thanks to the Lord for sending angels to protect them, no one was hurt. Another friend told me of a person who had a demon and began thrashing around. The friend asked the Lord to send angels to hold the demon down. "Suddenly it was as if there were four angels holding his arms and legs to the floor." Asking the Lord for angels to be at our disposal is an incredibly important request. I would never consider dealing with a home or person with demons without the knowledge that they 'had my back.'

# CHAPTER 7

~

## I Did All That And It Still Won't Leave

If you have done all of the things above and the ghosts/demons still haven't left then I would consider stepping back and asking the following questions...

### 1) Am I dealing with an entity that is much stronger than I first thought?

Sometimes when going into a home, you may not feel that the ghost is very strong. Any time you enter a home to cast out a ghost you are going in to do battle. One very old tactic in both earthly and spiritual armies is to make your enemy think you are powerless. This is why interviewing the residents of a home is so important. It gives you a good idea of what you'll be up against. Also we want to make sure that we prepare beforehand and have people praying for us as we are in the home.

### 2) Is there sin in your life or the life of someone in the house?

Prior to attempting to command a ghost to leave, it is necessary to be free of sin. Remember, any unconfessed, unforgiven sin in your life or the lives of those living in the home gives a right to Satan and his demons. They will exploit this and can at times be able to refuse to leave.

*neither give place to the devil.*

*Ephesians 4:27*

Another reason ghosts may be hesitant to leave was mentioned in the section on Prayer and Prayer Groups. If there is sin in a persons' life his prayers will not be heard by God. That conduit of communication must be open between you, those with you, and God.

*Behold, the Lord's hand is not shortened, that it cannot save; neither his ear heavy, that it cannot hear: but your iniquities have separated between you and your God, and your sins have hid his face from you, that he will not hear.*

*Isaiah 59:1,2.*

*If I regard iniquity in my heart, the Lord will not hear me.*

*Psalm 66:18.*

## 3) Do I Lack faith?

Faith is the belief in things yet unseen. It is to trust. If you have a problem trusting God to protect you or to make the ghosts leave, how can you expect them to go? It's almost like when animals can sense fear they are almost certain to attack. When, in the name of Jesus, you command a ghost to leave, don't have fear or doubt and they WILL leave.

When my son promises to clean his room, I have faith that he will get it done in a timely manner. There are those times that my son breaks his promise. God however, is trustworthy and will never fail to keep His promises.

*And God said unto Abraham, As for Sarai thy wife, thou shalt not call her name Sarai, but Sarah shall her name be. And I will bless her, and moreover I will give thee a son of her: yea, I will bless her, and she shall be a mother of nations; kings of peoples shall be of her. Then Abraham fell upon his face, and laughed, and said in his heart, Shall a child be born unto him that is a hundred years old? and shall Sarah, that is ninety years old, bear?*

*Genesis17:15-17*

*And Jehovah visited Sarah as he had said, and Jehovah did unto Sarah as he had spoken. And Sarah conceived, and bare Abraham a son in his old age, at the set time of which God had spoken to him.*

*Genesis 21:1-2*

If God can make a ninety year old woman who hadn't been able to conceive her entire life able to bear a child then certainly He is able to keep His promises to us.

*Know therefore that the LORD thy God, he is God, the faithful God, which keepeth covenant and mercy with them that love him and keep his commandments to a thousand generations*

*Deuteronomy 7:9*

*For therein is revealed a righteousness of God from faith unto faith: as it is written, But the righteous shall live by faith.*

*Romans 1:17*

*But the Lord is faithful, who shall stablish you, and keep you from evil.*

*2Theselonians 3:3*

# CHAPTER 8

*The Ghost Is Gone. Is There Something That Can Be Done To Keep It From Coming Back?*

When King Solomon finished building the first temple for God in Jerusalem and the priests finished consecrating it, the Holy Spirit of God descended as a cloud and moved in.

*And it came to pass, when the priests were come out of the holy place, that the cloud filled the house of Jehovah so that the priests could not stand to minister by reason of the cloud; for the glory of Jehovah filled the house of Jehovah. Then spake Solomon, Jehovah hath said that he would dwell in the thick darkness. I have surely built thee a house of habitation, a place for thee to dwell in for ever.*

*1Kings 8:10-13*

Once a demon has found a place to live it tends to want to stay. Once forcibly removed from a home, person or item, it leaves a void that must be filled because it will likely try to come back. It's amazing how often this happens when that void is left. When a demon returns he usually doesn't return alone and the situation becomes far worse than before.

*But the unclean spirit, when he is gone out of the man, passeth through waterless places, seeking rest, and findeth it not. Then he saith, I will return into my house whence I came out; and when he is come, he findeth it empty, swept, and garnished. Then goeth he, and taketh with himself seven other spirits more evil than himself, and they enter in and dwell there: and the last state of that man becometh worse than the first. Even so shall it be also unto this evil generation.*

*Matthew 12:43-45*

Once a demon has left, we need to pray over the place, person or item and ask God to fill that empty place with His Holy Spirit. By doing so, when the demon comes back he finds the place 'swept and garnished', but not empty. The last person a demon wants for a roommate is the Holy Spirit.

Also ask the Lord to send angels to watch over and protect the home. Many years ago, my dad went into every room of my parents' home and to each side of the property the house is on. He prayed, making a cross with olive oil over each door and pouring a little oil on the ground asking God to send angels to guard and protect the property and every person who comes into their home. He also asked the Holy Spirit to come live there. My dad passed away several years ago, but still, many people who have come to visit have commented on how warm and peaceful it feels there.

# In Summary

When God created the angels He gave them free wills, just as He gave us. We have a choice, accept the love God has for us and the forgiveness Jesus provided or reject them. There is no middle ground. Jesus said:

*He that is not with me is against me,*

*Matthew 12:30*

The angels had the same choice. But they had an advantage over us, they lived with God in heaven. They know firsthand the power, glory and love that God has. However, Lucifer became jealous when he found out that he was not going to be the highest creation for all eternity. He rebelled and convinced one third of the angels to join him in his quest to destroy mankind. He will do anything it takes to keep us away from the loving God he rejected.

Lucifer has commanded his fallen angels to deceive us in any way they can. Some of those ways are to make us think that there is an alternative to hell, such as purgatory and that hell does not exist. It's a lie that people who have passed away can come back as ghosts! Death seals our fate. We have up to the moment of death to ask God's forgiveness; after that is judgment. For the Christian it is a judgment unto reward for his service to God. For those that deny God's love and forgiveness it is a judgment unto punishment for their rejection.

Through the breaking of God's moral code we become bondservants, slaves to sin and the property of Satan. This gives him certain rights over us, over places where sins are committed and items used in the commission of those sins. One of those rights is the ability to possess a person, haunt a place or put a curse upon an object.

Although ancient rituals, sage burning, putting up crosses or crucifixes and quoting scriptures once in a while have some success in ridding homes and apartments of demons, they usually end up making things worse in the long run. Christians, those who have a *relationship* with God, have been given authority over fallen angels to cast them out of where they are living, permanently! It is extremely important to go into a home under the protection of God through prayer, forgiveness and wearing the whole armor of God.

> Put on the whole armor of God, that ye may be able to stand against the wiles of the devil. For our wrestling is not against flesh and blood, but against the principalities, against the powers, against the world-rulers of this darkness, against the spiritual hosts of wickedness in the heavenly places. Wherefore take up the whole armor of God, that ye may be able to withstand in the evil day, and, having done all, to stand. Stand therefore, having girded your loins with truth, and having put on the breastplate of righteousness, and having shod your feet with the preparation of

*the gospel of peace; withal taking up the shield of faith, wherewith*
*ye shall be able to quench all the fiery darts of the evil one. And*
*take the helmet of salvation, and the sword of the Spirit, which is*
*the word of God:*

*Ephesians 6:11-17*

If you bought this book because your home or a friend's home is haunted, I pray that what you have learned will help you. However, not all homes that have noises are haunted. If you are hearing odd things, the first thing I recommend is to have someone with good mechanical and plumbing skills check to see if there may be loose boards, banging pipes or drafts caused by poorly fitting windows. Once these have been ruled out then getting help from a pastor or a Christian who has experience dealing with ghosts/demons is the next step. If you, or someone you know, has a ghost in the home it should never be dealt with lightly. You should NOT try to take matters into your own hands. It has been my experience that ghosts should be forced to leave only by someone who knows Jesus, knows his or her authority through Him and preferably has experience dealing with ghosts/demons.

My advice to anyone with a ghost is to contact a local pastor who has a relationship with Jesus. Explain in as much detail as possible what has been going on in the home and ask the pastor to get a group together and to come pray, anoint the home and command the demons to leave 'in Jesus name.'

If you are a Christian and you bought this book in order to help others, then I pray that the Lord will bless your endeavors. However, I am NOT advocating going out and becoming a 'Ghostbuster!' Just remember, it's not you making demons leave, it's Jesus. Put on the full Armor of God and let the Lord lead you in all you do.

> *Now the God of hope fill you with all joy and peace in believing, that ye may abound in hope, in the power of the Holy Spirit.*
>
> *Romans 15:13*